THE CIT

'O

STOPPING SUICIDE ATTACKERS

THE CITIZEN'S GUIDE TO

STOPPING SUICIDE ATTACKERS

Secrets of an Israeli Counterterrorist

Itay Gil and Dan Baron
Paladin Press • Boulder, Colorado

The Citizen's Guide to Stopping Suicide Attackers:
Secrets of an Israeli Counterterrorist
by Itay Gil and Dan Baron

Copyright © 2004 by Itay Gil and Dan Baron

ISBN 10: 1-58160-433-5
ISBN 13: 978-1-58160-433-7
Printed in the United States of America

Published by Paladin Press, a division of
Paladin Enterprises, Inc.
Gunbarrel Tech Center
7077 Winchester Circle
Boulder, Colorado 80301 USA
+1.303.443.7250

Direct inquiries and/or orders to the above address.

PALADIN, PALADIN PRESS, and the "horse head" design
are trademarks belonging to Paladin Enterprises and
registered in United States Patent and Trademark Office.

Visit our Web site at www.paladin-press.com

Table of Contents

DISCLAIMER

The authors, publisher, and distributors of this book strongly discourage any illegal actions and/or behavior in connection with any of the information included in this book. The authors, publisher, and distributors of this book assume no responsibility or liability for errors or omissions in this book, or for any actions, including illegal actions, taken as a result of reading and/or using this book or the information contained herein. It is the reader's responsibility to research and comply with all applicable laws, including (but not limited to) laws regarding self-defense, use of force, and related topics. By reading this book and/or using or reviewing the information contained herein and/or by reading this disclaimer, you are agreeing to the terms of use contained in this disclaimer.

This book is presented *for academic study only.*

Introduction

HOW DO YOU DEAL with someone who wants, more than anything else in the world, to kill you and as many other people as possible? With men and women so twisted by fanatic hatred that they have decided to die while inflicting maximum casualties on innocent strangers? With contemporary terrorists who have no interest in negotiation and no fear of retaliation?

These are the quandaries faced by the entire civilized world since September 11, 2001.

Those 19 hijackers succeeded because they had the advantage of surprise—their mission was new to Americans more accustomed to hostage takers than suicidal attackers. And the terrorists knew it would be a devastatingly effective tactic because it had been tested elsewhere in the world. At least 11 groups actively use suicide as a weapon: two centered in the Palestinian territories, two in Egypt, and one each in Lebanon, Algeria, India, Sri Lanka, Turkey, Afghanistan, and Chechnya. Hundreds of suicide terrorist missions have taken place since 1981, and intelligence warnings predict the frequency will increase in coming years.

Suicide terrorism is devastating, yes, but not necessarily

unstoppable, as the brave souls of United Airlines Flight 93 proved. Because they made a concerted effort to fight back, they managed to end the hijacking and save an untold number of civilians on the ground.

The most lingering question is whether the passengers of Flight 93 had to die by crashing in that Pennsylvania field. Does confronting a suicide attacker necessarily mean sacrificing your life to save others?

The answer—and the underlying lesson of this book—is *no!*

This book will give you the tools necessary for a last-ditch stand against a suicide attacker, whether his weapon of choice is a knife, bomb belt, firearm, or even the front fender of his vehicle. Your objective will be to kill or at least subdue the terrorist before he does the same to you, no questions asked and no mercy shown.

Of course, the same principles must be applied to criminal threats—be it a violent junkie or mental patient, a madman on a shooting spree or an abusive spouse capable of committing murder—where the attacker has the same mentality as a suicide terrorist. The rule is this: If reason will not deter them from trying to take your life, they are terrorists who deserve to die.

While your survival in such dire situations can never be guaranteed 100 percent, by reading and absorbing the information in this book, you will be better prepared to confront the worst. This book will give you the knowledge and proper mind-set to stand up for yourself and your fellow citizens rather than just dumbly accept the cruel death someone else has imposed upon you. That is the right and the duty of all civilized human beings in the 21st century.

AUTHORS' NOTE

Although this book provides explicit instructions for close-combat techniques in specific situations, there is always the chance that they might not work exactly the way they are described or even it all. These techniques represent only one set of options based on our training and experience with Israeli police and military units, and they naturally cannot be duplicated exactly by everyone in all situations.

A fight to the death—and make no mistake about it, that's exactly what we are talking about in this book—is an inherently chaotic and unpredictable episode. When you attack a terrorist, you must realize that he will fight back. The most important lesson to learn from this book is to act decisively and, once committed, fight viciously and relentlessly. If the techniques described in the following chapters seem desperate or gruesome, remember that they are intended to be *last-ditch* efforts, when your only other choice is to submit to almost certain death.

1

Kamikaze Killers

MICHAEL CORLEONE: *I saw a strange thing today. Some rebels were being arrested. One of them pulled the pin on a grenade. He took himself and the captain of the command with him. Now, soldiers are paid to fight; the rebels aren't.*

HYMAN ROTH: *What does that tell you?*

MICHAEL CORLEONE: *It means they could win.*

from *The Godfather: Part II*
screenplay by Francis Ford Coppola and Mario Puzo

The suicide killers belong in a different psychic category, and their battle effectiveness has, on our side, no equivalent. Clearly, they have contempt for life. Equally clearly, they have contempt for death.

Novelist Martin Amis
writing in *The Guardian* newspaper, 9/18/2001

"KNOW YOUR ENEMY" is a common creed, but suicide attackers defy understanding.

How can you understand a man or woman who actively seeks violent self-destruction, flouting the human instinct for life? Conventional wisdom holds that suicide is a product of depression and defeat, yet these people kill themselves as part of what they consider a grand strategy. Some think they are earning heavenly reward by their actions, though all major religions condemn suicide.

"How could a normal human being do such a thing?" was the anguished cry of millions of Americans on September 11. That same, terrible wonderment racks Israelis after every Palestinian suicide bombing, and it was shared by Russians as they viewed television images of the Chechen rebels who seized the Moscow theater in an obvious dead-end mission in October 2002. Yet this is the enemy we must know in order to effectively respond to their murderous agenda.

Anger and a desire for retribution often follows any suicide attack. But here again the terrorists gain. Being extremists, they thrive on escalation. And because the direct perpetrator of the attack died (or, in the case of a bombing, literally disappeared) carrying it out, any retaliation cannot but seem, on some level, excessive. Robbed of a guilty party to punish, the victim country often goes for the terrorist's relatives or compatriots—witness Israel's policy of demolishing the family homes of suicide bombers. This generates even more hatred and wins new recruits for the terrorists.

Michael Corleone's observation on the pro-Castro insurgents in *The Godfather: Part II* says it all: Those who are willing to die for their cause, for whatever reason, are unstoppable. They could win.

But when you find yourself in the kill zone of a suicide bomber or buckled up in a passenger plane hurtling toward a city skyscraper, geopolitics will be the last thing on your mind. You will want to live. You will not want the terrorists to "win" by robbing you of your right to life. And the first step to beating them is understanding their background and motivation.

Suicide terrorism survives on its own sick mystique. Several factors reinforce a hostile mission in a foreign land, including the powerful grip of religious fanaticism, particularly when introduced to young, impressionable males; the step-by-step indoctrination into a culture of suicidal "martyrdom," which includes the making of goodbye videos as a form of diploma; and the way in which members of small groups interact.

Do not make the mistake of assuming that the suicide attack-

A Palestinian baby, dressed "festively" as a suicide bomber. (IDF Spokesman's Office)

er is insane. This may be the case with criminally violent junkies or mental patients, but it is rarely so with terrorists. They are murderous, yes, and certainly misguided, but they are almost never crazy. The discipline and preparation required for violent self-destruction makes the mentally unstable poor candidates. And the teamwork required for attacks such as 9/11 or the Moscow theater takeover rules out most forms of sociopathy. In fact, the psychological profile of a suicide terrorist more closely resembles that of a fanatical soldier or idealistic hunger striker than a lunatic killer.

Most suicide terrorists tend to be young, unmarried men with limited prospects for personal prosperity, but there are exceptions. The Tamil Tigers in Sri Lanka often use women for suicide attacks. Likewise, Kurdish rebels in Turkey pack explosives around the midsections of female volunteers so they appear pregnant and are spared body searches. More than a dozen Palestinian and Chechen women have struck in the same fashion. And the Arabic men who piloted the jetliners to their fiery ends on 9/11 were well out of their teens and, in at least one case, married and trained in a professional vocation.

The roots of self-destructive soldiering goes back at least to early Persia, when lone Muslim fighters in the 11th century launched dagger attacks on Christian Crusaders knowing they themselves would die. The attackers smoked hashish before setting out on their missions and were thus known as *hassasin* in Arabic, which evolved into the English word "assassin." There was also a famous episode in medieval Japan where the followers of a disgraced *shogun*, or military governor, carried out a retaliatory raid, then disemboweled themselves in accordance with ritual law.

In modern times, the use of suicide attacks has been associated almost exclusively with desperate causes. German pilots resorted to ramming their planes into bridges on the Eastern Front in a frantic and futile effort to stop the Russian advance at the end of World War II. Similarly, the Japanese resorted to kamikaze attacks when their nation was down to a skeletal air force and facing imminent Allied invasion. Kamikaze pilots were chosen from the elite, many of them university graduates. They felt obliged to sacrifice themselves because of a sense of duty to family and country. Most subscribed to the Shinto belief in eternal afterlife.

Suicide terrorism in the Middle East resumed in the 1980s, its proponents claiming that it was both a final-resort tactic against superior enemy armies and the highest achievement for Islamic warriors. During its war against Iraq in 1980–1988, Iran dressed teenage boys in burial shrouds, promised them martyr status, and sent them to their deaths in human-wave assaults. The first of several suicide bombers appeared in Lebanon in 1981 to protest Israel's military actions there. Among the early victims: 241 U.S. servicemembers killed in 1983 by a member of the Shiite group Hizbollah who rammed a bomb-laden truck into their Beirut barracks.

A Pakistani fan of Osama bin Laden and Saddam Hussein. The 9/11 suicide terrorists were psychologically fully formed adults who subordinated their individuality to the group. (Reuters)

Many Islamic clerics opposed the tactic as a violation of their faith. A notable exception was Hizbollah mentor Sheikh Fadlallah, who reasoned: "Well, you know, if you're going into battle and there's a 90 percent chance that you will die in this battle, you will go to the highest level of paradise. Well, if you go into battle knowing you will die and you're committing suicide, in effect, it's really only a matter of 10 percent and it's only a matter of timing. And they, too, should go to paradise because they're doing this for Allah and the sake of jihad."

Palestinian suicide bombings began in 1994, shortly after Israel and the Palestinian Authority signed peace deals meant to usher in a two-state coexistence. When hostilities resumed in September 2000, the number of attacks increased. This time, the terrorists went on suicidal shooting sprees in addition to carrying out bombings, with gunmen leaving behind the same valedictory videotapes. They tended to be about 20 years old and lacking in solid job prospects, unmarried and childless. At least one female suicide bomber was a divorcee, indicating her decision was as much an attempt to restore her family's "lost honor" as it was to strike a blow against the Israelis.

The Tamil Tigers, a largely secular group fighting for a separate ethnic state in Sri Lanka, launched its first suicide attack in 1987. Elite suicide warriors, equipped with cyanide capsules for use in the event of capture, conducted (and continue to conduct) regular raids against high-profile targets. In 1991, a female Tamil suicide bomber assassinated the former Indian premier, Rajiv Gandhi.

The Tamil Tigers have suicide recruits compete to be chosen for missions. The "winners" eat final meals with the charismatic leader of the movement, and photos of the celebrations are later released to local magazines. According to the leader's handbook, a suicide fighter must possess "a mind like steel but a heart like the petals of a flower."

The emphasis on psychological seasoning is common to other groups. The Palestinian groups Islamic Jihad and Hamas, for example, generally turn down first-time applicants, knowing they were probably driven by some triggering event such as the killing of a relative or friend by Israeli troops. But if the applicant keeps coming back, the recruitment process starts.

Those who are accepted undergo training and extensive indoctrination. They are assured that their families will be taken care of—often with generous stipends from Iran or Saudi Arabia—and that their act will win them special access to heaven. Famously, 72 virgins are said to be waiting in the afterlife. The terrorists consider their missions to be acts of martyrdom, not suicide.

But according to experts, religious zeal cannot by itself explain this brand of suicidal behavior.

"Two-thirds of [suicide] attacks in Lebanon were carried out by secular organizations," Ariel Merari, a psychologist at Tel Aviv University in Israel who has spent years studying suicide attacks around the world, said in a newspaper interview. "It's not an Islamic phenomenon. It's not a religious phenomenon. It's an organizational phenomenon."

A parallel can be seen with the Catholic hunger strikers in Northern Ireland, who knew that they were committing a mortal sin by starving themselves to death. But in order to attain their political objectives, the strikers had made a group pact that was inviolable.

Because the desire to participate in high-risk or suicidal missions dissipates with time, candidates are usually dispatched to their targets soon after they are selected and indoctrinated. Most groups don't allow prospective attackers to mingle with anyone outside the group's inner circle before an attack—and certainly not with the "enemy" lest they develop any degree of empathy or sympathy for their intended targets.

Yet the hijackers of 9/11 were different. They were not only slightly older and more educated than the typical suicide attacker, but they had sufficient mental stamina and emotional detachment to be in the United States for months and still hate Americans enough to kill them en masse.

"These people were living in the midst of Western life. No beard, no Qur'an, and yet they carry with them laser-like beams focusing on their ultimate missions. I see them as fully formed psychological adults who have subordinated their individuality to the group," Jerrold Post, a former CIA psychological profiler, told National Public Radio.

Experts believe these men were kept on their long-term pro-

Three New York City firemen end their shift at Ground Zero,
September 12, 2001. (Reuters)

ject through tight group control, with the four or five men in each cell serving as a mutually reinforcing small community.

"Suicidal terrorist attacks are not a matter of individual whim," said Merari. "I don't know of a single case in which an individual decided on his or her own to carry out a suicidal attack. In all cases—it certainly is true in Lebanon and Israel and Sri Lanka and the Kurdish case—it was an organization that picked the people for the mission, trained them, decided on the target, chose a time, arranged logistics, and sent them."

And therein lies another major motivator for the terrorists: peer pressure. As in military boot camp, their sense of self and individuality are subordinated as their identity is merged into the identity of the group. For a would-be suicide attacker to think of his own life would seem, well, *selfish*.

The group dynamic can also deter any individual who wants to back out at the last moment. He not only would face the wrath of the shadowy leaders who planned the operation, but he would be led to believe that he would be letting down his immediate circle of friends, peers, and comrades.

"Suicide candidates, when they are chosen by an organization, enter into one end of a production process and on the other end they come out as complete, ready suicides," said Merari. "From that point on he is already dead, mentally and in the eyes of his comrades. He cannot go back."

What this also means is that there are—in the United States and abroad—ticking human time bombs. They are the living dead—recruited, trained, committed—biding their time until they are commanded to carry out their deadly missions.

The only question that remains is whether you can spot them in time to fight . . . and survive.

2

Terminal Touch

FOR CIVILIANS UNSCHOOLED in the arts of close-quarters combat, taking on a suicide terrorist hand-to-hand is a daunting, even unthinkable, prospect. Faced with a fanatic bent on killing and dying, most people will feel their willpower ebb at the thought of confronting this breed of human being. At best, most will pluck up the courage to flee.

But as will be seen in upcoming chapters, sometimes a fight is unavoidable. If so, it must be quick and decisive in your favor. You never know what detonator, gun, or hidden reserves of murderous energy the terrorist has, so you have to know how to put him down for good.

Here are some of our favorite, all-purpose moves. There are many others available to anyone who takes the time to familiarize him or herself with practical, no-nonsense combatives.

THE PEN PUSHER

Keep a pen on you at all times. When the assailant grabs you, lock down his hand with one of your hands, then stab him in the soft inside part of the wrist with the other (fig. 1). Better yet, go straight for the throat if possible (fig. 2).

Figure 1

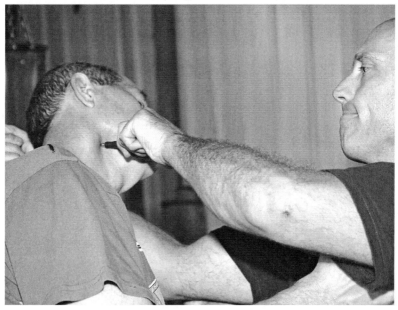

Figure 2

LOWER-BODY KICKS

A hard kick to the groin is worth trying, but it is a common myth that it is a guaranteed fight stopper. It's not. Knees, however, are great targets because they are fragile and, if damaged, will immobilize the terrorist (fig. 3). If he's sprawled on the ground with a wrecked knee, he cannot continue with his murderous agenda. Once he's on the ground, keep kicking and stomping on him if the opportunity presents itself. Other good targets include the head, face, throat, weapon arm, and shins (to further immobilize him). Do not let up.

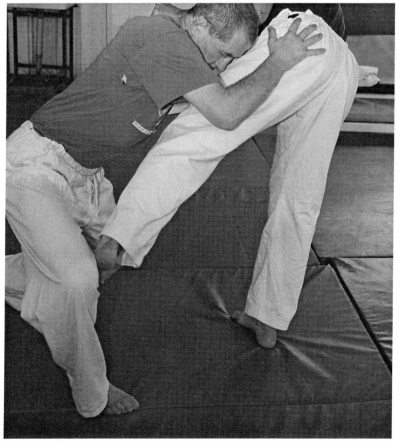

Figure 3

THROAT STRIKES

Even the most seasoned of terrorists is liable to forget the boxer's cardinal rule: keep your chin down. Go for your assailant's throat and you are as guaranteed to stop him as with any other move. A fist with palm turned upward will help you to penetrate under the chin (fig. 4), or strike with the web of your hand between your thumb and index finger to get a broader crushing surface. You can also flatten your fist and curl your knuckles tightly to better penetrate to his throat.

With a crushed windpipe, the terrorist is likely to flail and will possibly try to grapple with you. Use your other arm to fend him off as you continue to strike him until he is incapacitated. If he has a knife or gun, you must mind his weapon arm always, even if you think you've delivered a fatal blow! (More on this important concept later.)

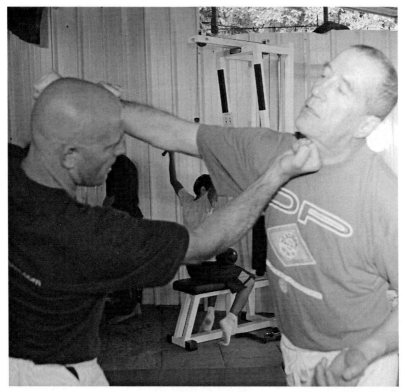

Figure 4

NOSE MASH

Mash the terrorist's nose with the meat of your palm (fig. 5). The blow will temporarily obscure his sight as he tears up involuntarily. (Don't believe stories you may have heard about instant death from bone cartilage penetrating the brain—that's extremely rare.) Use your free arm to fend off his attacks or, if you are already in grappling mode, to keep him in place as you continue to pound on him.

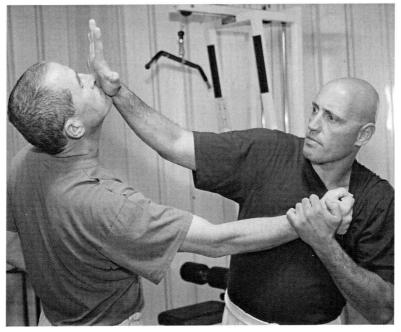

Figure 5

EYE GOUGE, CHEEK RIP

Self-explanatory. Let him feel some terror for a change (figs. 6, 7)! If you go for the cheek rip, beware of the possibility of the terrorist biting down on your fingers. Keep them clear of his teeth!

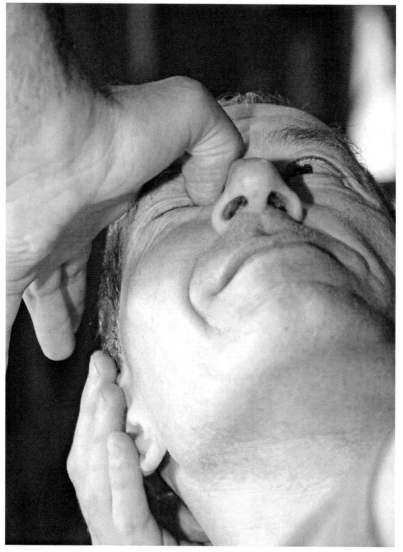

Figure 6

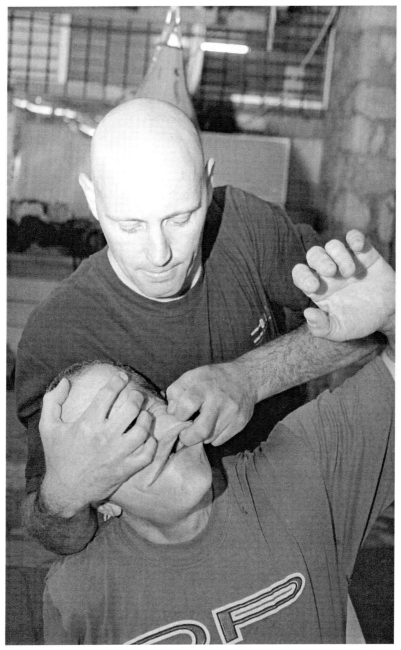

Figure 7

FOOT SWEEP

If you can approach the terrorist from behind, this is a great way to get him to drop whatever weapons he might have. Swept off his feet, his instinct will be to reach forward and block his fall. Even if he maintains a grip on his weapon, you still have put him on the ground, where he cannot continue his assault and will be easier to subdue.

To effect the foot sweep, quickly come up behind the suspect and drop to one knee, sliding close to his legs. If your hands are powerful enough, grab his ankles; if not, then hook the elbow of your strong arm around both ankles. Then yank hard (fig. 8), rising to your feet and bucking backwards.

Figure 8

3

The Highest Stakes

YOU WOULD THINK that, after the atrocities of 9/11, no terrorist would be stupid enough to attempt another suicide hijacking.

Think again.

In November of 2002, 23-year-old Tawfiq Fukra boarded an El Al flight from Tel Aviv to Istanbul. According to witnesses, as the plane was landing he stormed toward the cockpit, using a pocketknife to slash a stewardess who tried to block his way. He was subdued by two sky marshals after a brief scuffle and, according to Turkish authorities, later confessed to planning to commandeer the plane, turn it around, and ram it into a skyscraper in Israel. He would not say how he managed to smuggle the knife aboard.

A close call. Too close, given El Al's legendary security. And other airlines have yet to meet even that standard, for all the precautions instituted after 9/11. Suicide hijackers could well strike again because the tactic is just too tempting. In the hands of a terrorist, a passenger jet becomes both a death trap for hundreds of civilians on board and a makeshift ballistic missile that can destroy ground targets with perfect aim. Of course, passengers aboard buses or trains are almost as vulnerable and in need of precaution.

American Airlines # 11

Al Suqami   Waleed M. Alshehri   Wail M. Alshehri   Alomari   Atta

Mohammed Atta, et al. More in store? (Reuters)

But one factor has changed since 9/11: the nature of human fear. The attacks on the World Trade Center and Pentagon worked mainly because the passengers acquiesced to the terrorists, believing that they were being taken hostage and would eventually be released. Their paralyzing fear seemed reasonable. But those on United Flight 93 knew otherwise. They knew that by yielding to a gang of men wielding cardboard cutters, they were merely making themselves easy kills. "Let's roll!" was their declaration that fear was not an option.

LONE RISKS

Remember this whenever you fly. The speed of the plane, the sensitivity of its controls, the volatility of its fuel, and the vulnerability of its crew all mean that you will have precious seconds to intervene if the nightmare scenario comes true (fig. 9). In all likelihood you will not be alone in fighting back, but do not count on it. You are only accountable for your own life, and ultimately you are responsible for safeguarding it.

Think defensively before you board. First, request an aisle seat. This will give you the option of movement should a crisis occur. Sitting in the middle or by the window may give you some initial protection from the hijackers' knives, but ultimately you will feel trapped and devoid of any control of your own fate. The passengers on either side of you will have unwittingly become your jailers, keeping you confined to your seat.

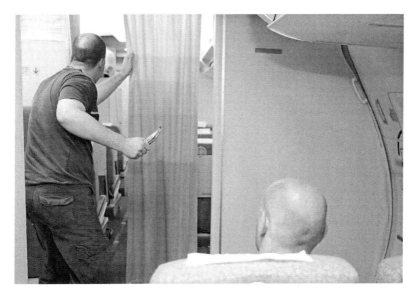

Figure 9

That's doubly bad, because your fellow passengers are your potential allies in overpowering hijackers. Keep this in mind when you first come aboard. Make eye contact with those sitting close to you. Introduce yourself and learn their names. It will come in handy if you have to shout out to them for help.

For the same reason, you should size up these potential allies for the attributes necessary to wage a fight against armed hijackers. Physical fitness and latent aggression are important, but noticing these is a matter of instinct, not science. Bodyweight is far easier to gauge, and "mass attack" is crucial to overwhelming the terrorists. So look out for heavy hitters. Generally, these individuals will be adult men, but not necessarily. A hefty woman will be just as much of a handful for the hijacker.

Also take the time to scan the other passengers for would-be bad guys. Look out especially for Middle Eastern-looking men who appear to be traveling alone. Do not waste time chiding yourself for "racial profiling"—you are acting reasonably, given the fact that a disproportionate amount of terrorism, including the events of 9/11, has emanated from Arab countries. If you are discreet enough, no one should take offense (fig. 10).

Once the worst happens, banish any sense of discretion from your mind. Although you will naturally want to save the lives of your fellow passengers as well as your own, in a fast-moving, life-or-death situation, you cannot afford the luxury of being overly concerned with the risks posed to others during your confrontation with the terrorists. It is believed that some of the 9/11 hijackers succeeded by holding a knife to the throat of a stewardess or passenger in order to force the crew to open up the cockpit, which they did. One person was saved—only to be incinerated along with everyone else minutes later. Not a good trade-off.

Do not let this happen to you. If a terrorist threatens a passenger or member of the cabin staff, do not give in or expedite the hijacking in any way. If this means that the hostage gets his or her throat slashed, it will have to be an unfortunate outcome of an already horrible situation. In stark terms, it is a reasonable loss when compared to the 100 percent casualty rate the terrorists intend.

Of course, the situation is different if you are the one taken hostage, which could occur if you decided to sit in the aisle. If that

Figure 10

happens, your fight reflex should kick in immediately. Do not count on others to come to your aid. Assume you are facing imminent death—alone.

KNIFE ESCAPE, SEATED

A hijacker could put a knife to your throat while you are seated, either to force you on your feet and take you toward the cockpit or as a preamble to killing you. Hijackers will most likely go for the throat rather than torso because (A) their weapons will be makeshift (e.g., box cutters) and therefore only effective against exposed skin, and (B) a slashed throat is a quick way to terrorize an entire cabin of passengers into submission.

The hijacker's non-weapon hand should be less of a concern to you. Yes, he can and likely will use it to subdue or fight you, especially once you resist. He may, in the savageness of the fight, tear your hair, claw your eyes, or punch your face repeatedly with his free hand, so you must be aware of and prepared for this eventuality. In order to depict the counterattack techniques clearly, however, we have not tried to capture this likelihood in the photos. You, of course, should do your best to avoid or minimize the damage if he does attack you with his free hand (for example, keep your chin tucked firmly to protect your vulnerable throat), but as far as you are concerned, his knife hand is all that is important. (For the sake of the demonstration, we will assume his left hand is his knife hand and that you are sitting right of the aisle, although these techniques work just as well in any other permutation.)

Of course, there is the not inconsequential matter of the seat belt to consider. On the one hand, it is a mandatory piece of safety equipment, especially during takeoffs and landings. On the other hand, it will seriously impede your movements should you have to tussle with terrorists.

The decision to unbuckle once airborne is up to you and will largely depend on to what extent you sense a potential threat aboard after having scanned the surroundings. Turbulence will also be a factor in weighing whether to leave your seat belt fastened. If you keep it on, always keep the buckle exposed and easy to reach should you need to move quickly.

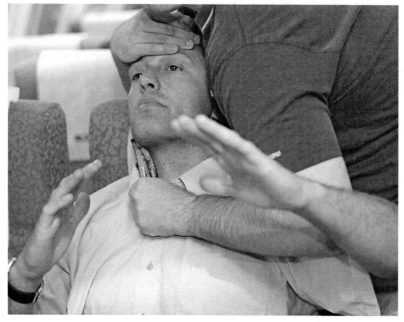

Figure 11

The hijacker might put the knife point to the exposed left side of your neck, but for a greater sense of control he may very well reach over to the right, as though about to jerk the knife across and slit your throat (fig. 11). Whatever the case, your response will be the same: pulling his knife hand across (i.e., stretching out his arm) to clear the blade of your throat rather than trying to push it away. This motion might run against instinct in such situations, but it will momentarily trap the weapon hand and surprise the attacker enough to earn you a second's advantage.

As soon as you feel the knife against your neck, buck backwards into your seat while clamping the hijacker's elbow with your left hand or arm (fig. 12) and grasping his wrist with your right hand (fig. 13). Then sink down while sliding forward. Keep forcing his weapon arm (and him) toward the window, clearing the aisle for your next course of action and keeping him confined between the seats if possible. The passenger to your left might get cut in all the thrashing, but it is unlikely to be lethal and, as discussed above, such collateral damage is acceptable.

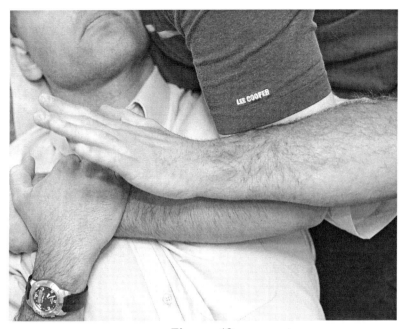

Figure 12

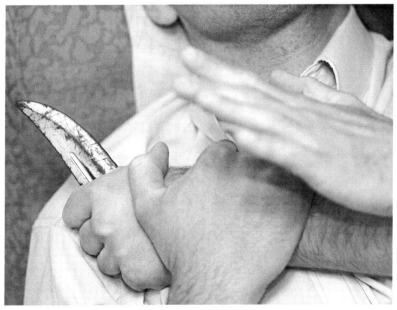

Figure 13

By the end of this stage, you will find yourself almost flat on your back, knees jammed into the seat in front, and the hijacker sprawled over you (fig. 14). Your combined sizes might make it impossible for you (and he) to extricate yourself, but this is still an acceptable outcome because (A) he no longer can slit your throat, and (B) he has lost the element of surprise, not to mention his balance, and now will hopefully have to deal with several responding passengers.

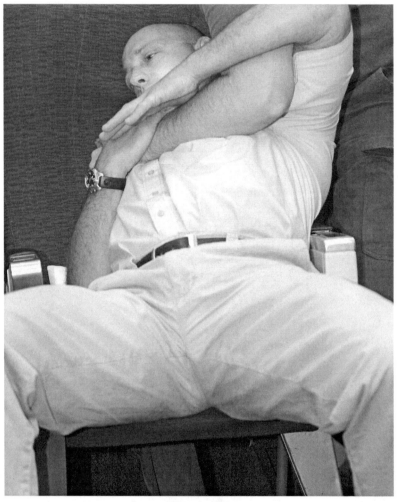

Figure 14

Should you still be able to move, you can finish him off yourself. Keeping hold of his arm, continue to slide out of your seat until you are kneeling on the floor, rear end in the aisle (figs. 15, 16).

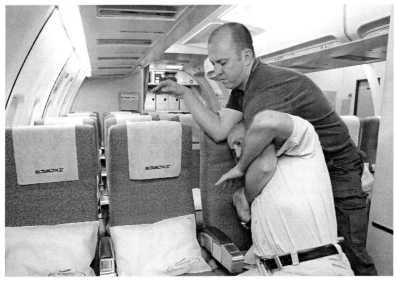

Figure 15

Figure 16

You now have his weapon arm twisted (fig. 17), and wriggling out and rising to your feet (fig. 18) will hopefully be enough to pin him down with the rear of his head and neck exposed for debilitating punches, elbows, and forearm strikes.

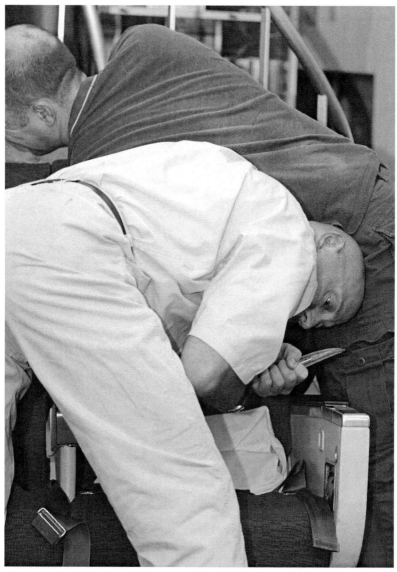

Figure 17

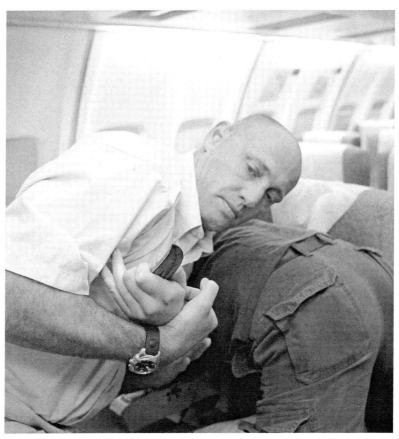

Figure 18

If he is still holding the knife, you can perform a pain-compliance wrist lock by placing your palm on the back of his hand and forcefully bending his wrist toward his elbow (fig. 19), or sharply bend back and break his fingers so he releases the knife (fig. 20).

During this struggle, you might very well get cut as the hijacker resists your efforts and fights back. Although it is obviously something you want to avoid, you might even instinctually grab the sharp blade itself or end up with your hand around it in your desperation to control his weapon hand. Ignore the pain; think of your hand as a safety buffer earning you the extra seconds you need to win the fight. If you get cut in this or any other way, never let it stop you from savagely and relentlessly pressing your assault.

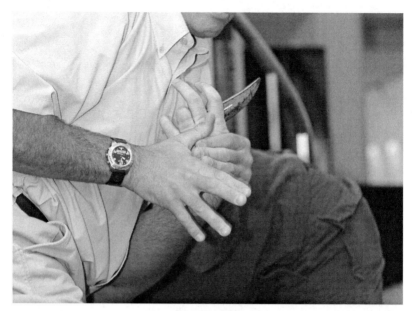

Figure 19

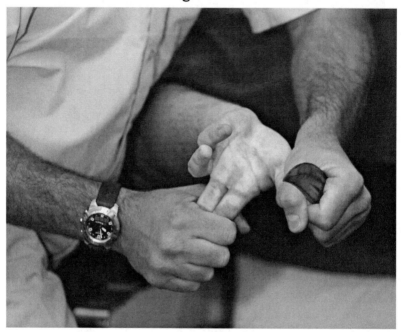

Figure 20

THE CITIZEN'S GUIDE TO STOPPING SUICIDE ATTACKERS

KNIFE ESCAPE, STANDING, FROM BEHIND

To save time, the hijacker may try to take someone hostage who is already standing and therefore can be led more easily and quickly toward the cockpit. Stewardesses are especially vulnerable to this, since the hijacker realizes that the crew knows her and are more likely to be affected by threats to her life. This gives crucial leverage to the terrorists.

As a standing target, the terrorist will come at you either from the front or rear. In either case, he will try to force you to lead him down the aisle—dragging is too difficult and time-consuming.

When attacking from behind, the hijacker may go for the same knife lock as discussed above, except this time he will have freer use of his non-weapon hand (fig. 21). Although you must be aware that this hand is not immobile and that he can do damage with it, you must pay it no heed. Focus on dominating and neutralizing his knife arm.

Figure 21

Again, surprise the attacker by grasping his knife arm by the elbow and wrist and pulling it across you. But here, instead of ducking straight down, bend over at the waist as though initiating a judo flip (fig. 22). Once your head is at his armpit level (your body should be at about a 90 degree angle; fig. 23), take a step back so you are clear of his body. Keep a firm grip on his arm throughout.

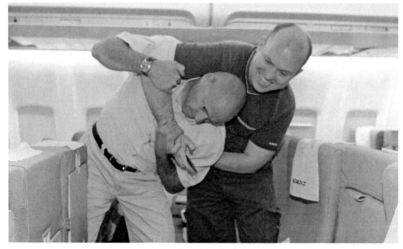

Figure 22

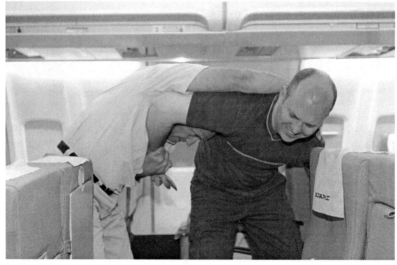

Figure 23

You now have the hijacker in a classic armlock (fig. 24). To pin him to the seat or floor, all you need to do is raise his arm a little to inflict serious pain on his joints. You can also expedite the process of getting him to the floor by stomping on the backs of his knees. Should he tumble into a seat, you can pummel him there, using the metal seat belt buckle as an improvised weapon if it is accessible (fig. 25).

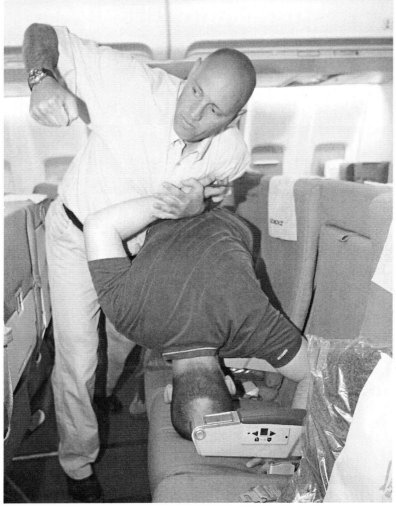

Figure 24

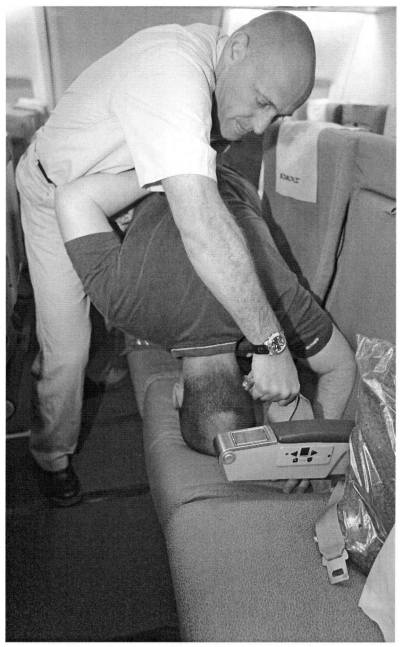

Figure 25

A simpler method of resistance is to bite the weapon hand after clearing the knife from your throat (fig. 26). This is ideal for women or other passengers who may feel uncertain of their ability to man-handle the attacker as described above. Bite viciously and deep, and don't let go.

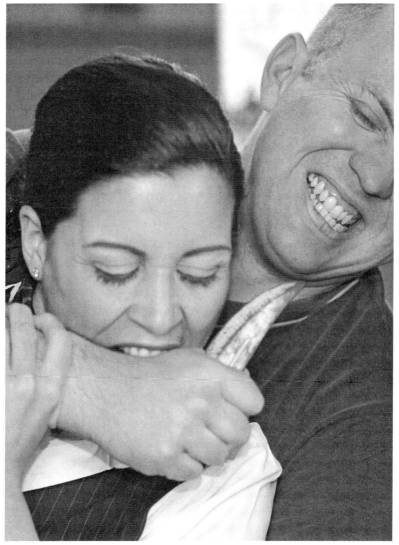

Figure 26

KNIFE ESCAPE, STANDING, FROM THE FRONT

We've all seen those films where a mugger accosts his victim by grabbing his lapel with one hand and waving a knife in his face with the other (fig. 27). It may seem cliché, but this is indeed the instinctive way to threaten someone with this sort of weapon. They think (and not without reason) that by controlling the victim's neck area, they can control his body entirely; flash a blade near his throat and they control his will too. By subverting that submission reflex, you can turn the tables on an attacker who tries this grip on you.

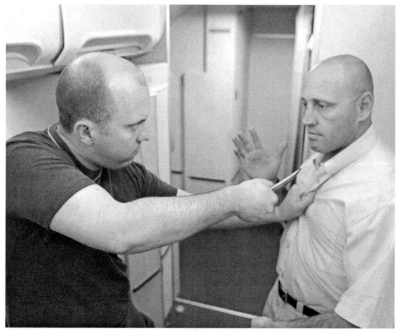

Figure 27

Unlike a mugger, a hijacker will not want to keep you in place but rather will want to walk you backwards, leading him toward the cockpit. This works to your advantage because you can anticipate his momentum and use it against him when you counterattack.

Take a few steps with him to make him think you are complying (fig. 28)—but not too many or you will begin to lose your balance and, with it, any chance of gaining physical control of the

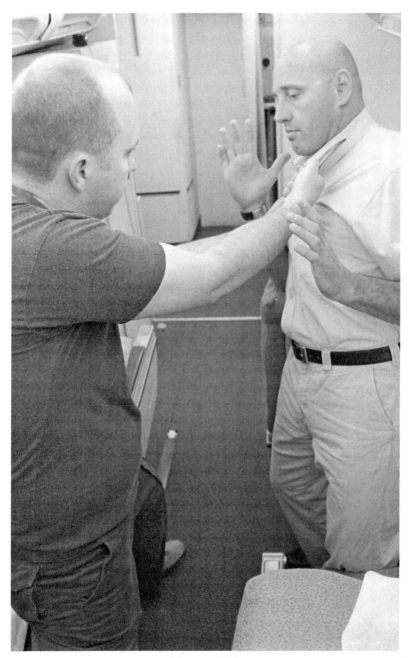

Figure 28

situation. After your third or fourth step, take another, larger one that will force the hijacker to lurch forward in order to keep up. At the same time, bring your right hand up to grab and pin his left (the one holding you by the lapel). With your left hand, grab his right (holding the knife; fig. 29) and slam it down sideways so that the blade slices his left forearm (fig. 30).

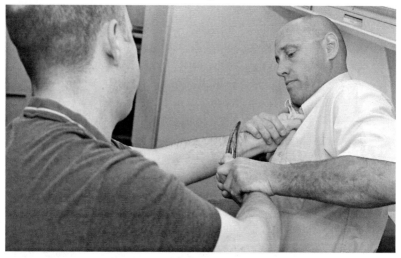

Figure 29

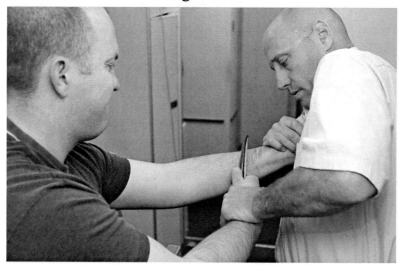

Figure 30

If the cut is deep enough, it will cause severe bleeding and possibly sever some nerves, making his left hand open involuntarily. Even if the damage is less, the hijacker should be sufficiently stunned to allow you and fellow passengers to subdue him.

Once the weapon is controlled, try all the standard unarmed techniques—kicks to the groin, knees, and shins; gouges to the eyes; strikes to the throat—anything to incapacitate him. The only rule at this point is that there are no rules. Show no mercy until the man is incapable of carrying through with his assault.

THE AIRLINE ARSENAL

Your average airliner offers ample opportunity to fashion makeshift weapons of your own. Here are some ideas. There are literally dozens of others.

The next time you board an airplane, look around and locate as many improvised weapons as you can. Remember: Not only will you need a weapon, but your fellow passengers will too. You should perform this mental exercise every time you fly.

Belt Garrote

Your belt can make a great garrote. Remove it as discreetly as possible, then grab both ends, ideally with one hand palm up and the other palm down (fig. 31). Approach the hijacker from

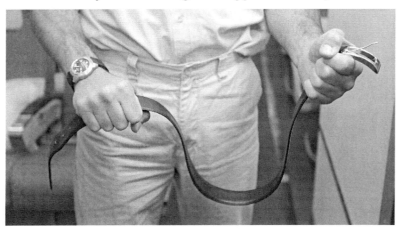

Figure 31

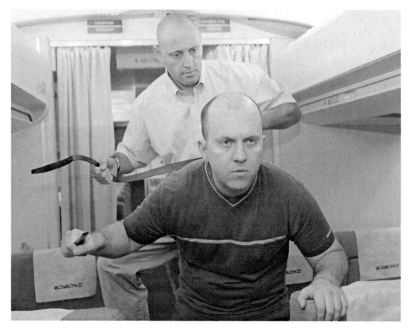

Figure 32

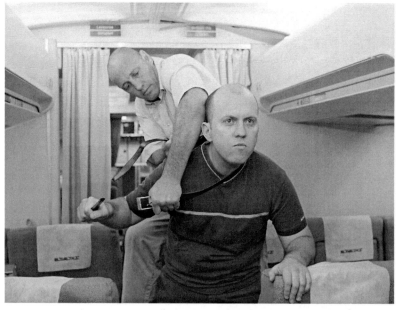

Figure 33

behind (fig. 32), positioning the palm-down end of the belt behind his head, then quickly wrap the belt around his neck with the palm-up end (fig. 33). This grip will give you maximum squeeze as you tighten the noose (fig. 34). To end it quick, place one knee in the small of the terrorist's back and pull backwards with both hands (fig. 35).

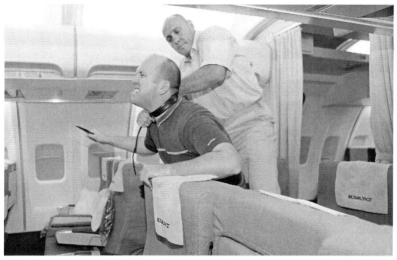

Figure 34

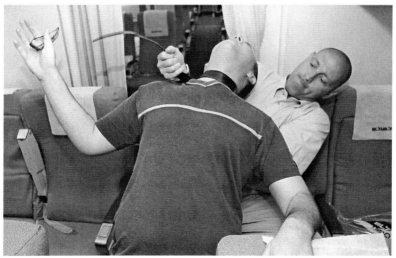

Figure 35

The hijacker will not passively submit to your choking attack. He will likely attempt to twist around and stab you, or he will slash wildly at your exposed arms and hands holding the garrote. If there is room in the confined space of the cabin, as you pull backward you can try to twist the hijacker around and slam him face first to the floor. By simultaneously choking him while wrenching him to the ground, it may prevent him from having the physical control and presence of mind to slash you with his uncontrolled weapon hand.

Meal Trays

Meal trays are light but robust, ideal for crushing a hijacker's windpipe. Hold it in both hands and, starting from the middle of your chest, shove upward at his throat (fig. 36). The same effect can be achieved with the rigid plastic sleeve covering the magazines that are usually found in the seat pocket in front of you or in narrow side bins in the front and back of the plane.

Figure 36

Soda Can Knife

Soda cans can be turned into makeshift blades. Twist the can so it tears in two (do so as discreetly as possible under your fold-down meal tray; fig. 37), then fashion it into a pointed and/or bladed implement (fig. 38) and stomp on it to flatten it. Pay special attention to flattening the jagged edges against one another so you end up with a thicker, sturdier weapon. Depending on how the weapon turns out, you can use it as a slashing implement or a push dagger. It's a good idea to practice making these weapons at home so you will not have to waste precious time experimenting under the intense pressure of a hijack crisis.

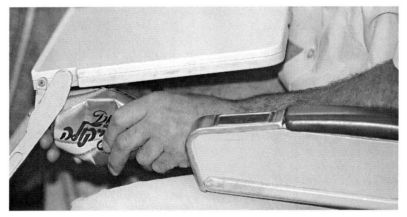

Figure 37

Figure 38

Hot Water

Take advantage of the scalding water on hand. Every airliner cabin has a kitchen compartment with an instant hot-water dispenser or where the staff keeps a kettle on the boil. Throwing this water in a hijacker's face will do a lot to cool him down (fig. 39). This tactic reportedly was used by the passengers on Flight 93.

Figure 39

GANG UP

There is ultimately no more effective tactic to use against hijackers than sheer superior numbers. Think about it: You passengers will outnumber most any group of hijackers by at least fifty to one. By dint of collective bodyweight, you can beat them in seconds. Whether you are the one who rouses the crowd or the one who answers someone else's call to arms, do so knowing that there is no alternative. One or more of you could get hurt or worse, but it is better than the total devastation that the terrorists have in store for everyone.

4

The Hidden Threat

SUICIDE BOMBERS are becoming an international scourge. Palestinian terrorists, Tamil Tigers, Hezbollah fighters, and Kurdish and Chechen separatists are all increasingly resorting to this devastating tactic. The United States has, so far, been spared—but intelligence warnings indicate this is but a temporary delay. In such films as *The Siege* and *To Live and Die in L.A.*, Hollywood has had no trouble anticipating a time in the near future when human bombs hold entire American cities hostage.

The principle is simple. In the words of one Israeli demolitions expert, "Suicide bombers are like miniature cruise missiles, only much smarter." The attacker is dispatched to a target area, penetrates its most crowded point, and detonates a bomb hidden on his or her person. That's how a Tamil terrorist assassinated Indian premier Rajiv Gandhi in 1991—by placing herself among a group of spectators receiving him on an official visit and waiting for him to reach her before detonating her load. She even bowed first to make sure Gandhi was looking at her face-on when he took the brunt of the blast.

The extent of the kill zone, of course, depends on the type of explosives used. The Kurds favor simply running at their targets

The aftermath of a suicide bombing aboard a Jerusalem bus. (Reuters)

with primed hand grenades, but this tactic is not designed for extensive penetration and the damage is limited. The Palestinians, meanwhile, have used everything from ground-up matchstick heads mixed with gasoline to bootleg C-4. Nuts, bolts, ball bearings, and metal shards are mixed in as shrapnel. The total weight of the payload is usually between 10–30 lbs. (about 5kg and 15kg), enough to pack a lethal punch but no so heavy as to burden the bomber, who is, after all, meant to look like a regular pedestrian.

The bomb can be carried in a backpack or strapped on the body with a belt or vest. The detonator is always within the terrorist's reach. Sometimes it is a standard electrical switch carried in the palm of the bomber's hand and pressed at the critical moment. Other times it is a plunger button on the surface of the bomb that can be slammed down from outside the clothes or bag material without having to be touched directly.

And that is where the suicide bomber's main vulnerability lies—his or her hands. This chapter will cover several techniques for subduing and killing the terrorist, all of them based on this rule.

A WORD FOR ARMED DEFENDERS

Suicide bombers have one goal: to die while killing as many innocent people as possible. This leaves defenders no choice but to kill them as quickly and cleanly as possible. Clearly, an armed response by authorized and trained gun owners is ideal.

Contrary to teachings in many gun academies, suicide bombers must be shot in the head and never the torso. The head is a smaller and more difficult target, but in this situation it is actually less risky to go for it. Consider that in October 2002, a group of Israeli soldiers overpowered a Palestinian would-be suicide bomber in the West Bank, and all would have been well had not a concerned citizen come up and shot the terrorist in the abdomen. The bullet apparently set off the bomb belt, and three Israelis died along with the bad guy.

Equally important, a shot to the head maximizes your chances for instant incapacitation. Any experienced street cop could tell you of instances where criminals have been shot multiple times in the torso, only to continue on their rampage.

Bulky clothes, protruding wires (bomb is shown fully exposed for illustrative purposes), a "lock-on" look—Is he a suicide bomber?

SPOTTING THEM IN TIME

With few exceptions, suicide bombers are by definition covert, posing as normal civilians until the point of detonation. They can be men or women, young or old, dressed as friendly military servicemen or as ultrafashionable teens. They can arrive at their target on foot, in a car, or even by bicycle.

Identifying suicide bombers in time is the toughest challenge facing security forces everywhere, and the giveaway traits change from country to country and culture to culture. But there are several universal clues to look out for:

- *Unseasonably bulky clothes,* especially winter coats. If the guy is sweating, he is overdressed. He could be concealing a bomb belt.
- *Mismatched apparel.* Look out for military or civilian uniforms that are missing insignia or crucial bits of equipment. The

Palestinians have sent out bombers disguised as Israeli soldiers without giving them guns. (Why waste good hardware?) In Israel, a rifleman without a rifle is an oddity.

- *Bomb bits.* Electrical wires do not ordinarily jut out from the bottom of someone's backpack, sleeve, or shirt. Suicide bombers' devices are often primitive affairs and not packed well. They don't have to be. If those wires look designed to be within easy reach of the suspect's hands, go into action before he does.

- *Erratic behavior.* Is the suspect walking around alone, indecisively, as if he does not know whether to proceed or how? Is he scratching at his clothes or shifting his bag from hand to hand? Could be he is having second thoughts about his mission. For every successful suicide bomber, there are a handful of others who either backed out at the last moment or made sure they were caught by security forces and thus saved their own lives. This is not to say that the guy you are monitoring won't go through with it just because he's acting erratic or indecisive.

- *The "lock-on" look.* Security guards at several Israeli establishments who have survived suicide bombings described the terrorist meeting their eyes and walking toward them before blowing up. There could be several explanations for this behavior. The bomber may have been trying to defuse the guard's suspicions by seeming friendly long enough to carry out the attack. Or he could have targeted the guard because he saw that civilians were keeping close to him for a sense of security, therefore making the guard and his surroundings the best area to hit.

But there could be a deeper psychological motivation. Suicide bombers carry out their drastic act out of hatred and anger as well as, for some, a belief that they are fulfilling a religious duty for which they will be rewarded. At the point of detonation, they want to know they are hitting the "enemy" despite all his precautions, and this means targeting symbols of national defense. Servicemen and even security guards fit the bill.

The advantage of this cocky last act is that it gives the guard a chance to react. In May 2002, the doorman of a Jerusalem café spotted the lock-on look of a suicide bomber in time to push him outside and hit the deck. Eleven people died, but the carnage would have been far worse had the terrorist detonated inside.

LAST CHANCE!

Before discussing techniques for stopping suicide bombers, it is important to emphasize that these techniques are lethal, and the potential for tragic mistakes is very real. If the political climate is such that suicide bombings are a real and present danger, you are fully within your rights to exercise self-defense and engage suspicious individuals. But at the outset of the confrontation, leave a little room to disengage if you realize you are mistaken. If you have grabbed the suspect and he or she does or says something that proves there is nothing to fear, then back off. It could be that the suspicious behavior was in fact a sign of mental illness or due to some more innocuous reason. Real suicide bombers rarely protest their innocence or beg for their lives once they have decided to act.

Obviously, suicide bomber scenarios are extremely dangerous. You must size up these situations in an instant and act decisively. If, however, you have no realistic chance of reaching the bomber and subduing him before he can detonate his device, your only option might be to shout an alarm to other bystanders and dive for cover.

BOMB BELTS

Bomb belts take the form of girdles worn low on the abdomen or vests that cover the entire chest. As long as the terrorist can reach the front of his torso, he can reach the hidden switch that will detonate the explosives.

If you have a partner to help you engage the terrorist, do so simultaneously. Whether you approach him from the front or rear, it is important to be especially stealthy so you do not alert him to your intentions. When you make your move, it is vital that you act with lightning speed. Once you have immobilized his arms and the grappling is underway, start shouting "bomb!" to warn others to clear the area.

Each of you secures one of the terrorist's arms, catching it across your chest and trapping the forearm around your rib cage (fig. 40). Next, each of you kicks out the leg closest to you so the terrorist falls on his back (fig. 41). Stay with him as he goes to the ground.

Figure 40

Figure 41

It must be emphasized that the would-be bomber needs to be taken to the ground on his back rather than his front (fig. 42). If he is thrust down on his face, there is a possibility that the detonator could slam into the ground and set off the device. There was even a case outside Jerusalem where a suicide bomber was spread-eagled face down by police, who then shot him when they realized he was trying to rub the detonator switch on the ground.

Figure 42

Once you have him on the ground with his arms still trapped, use your inside elbow and fist to pummel his head (fig. 43), focusing on his temples. Keep doing this until he loses consciousness or an armed civilian or security officer comes up to shoot him. Crushing his throat is another effective quick-kill method. In any case, never let go of his arms until you are absolutely certain he can no longer reach the bomb detonator.

Figure 43

After the terrorist has been subdued, you and your partner should get up, run a distance of 10–20 feet (4–5 meters), then hit the deck, crossing your legs and covering your head in case the bomb belt blows up. Wait for 10 seconds, then crawl away quickly and await the arrival of the authorities.

If you are tackling the suicide bomber alone, you must be even more subtle and speedy. Approach him from the front as if you were going to pass him on his side. Do not make eye contact—let him think you are just a passerby.

As you come up alongside, thrust your hand into the crook of the arm (fig. 44) whose hand is out of sight (in a pocket, for example), then swing around the terrorist's back to grab his other arm in the same way (fig. 45). (Speed and the element of surprise are essential here.) Bring your hands together into the small of his back and, using both, grab the clothes at the base of his neck or lock up his upper arms (fig. 46). You now have him in a tight armlock.

Figure 44

Figure 45

The Citizen's Guide to Stopping Suicide Attackers

Figure 46

Aiming at the backs of his knees, kick out his legs from behind (fig. 47). When the terrorist crumples, lead him backwards so that he falls in a seated position (fig. 48). He may fall to his side during the struggle; if so, do not let his front plane make contact with the floor or another part of his body. In general, pay attention to what he's trying to do or where on his body he's trying to access and prevent him from doing so.

Figure 47

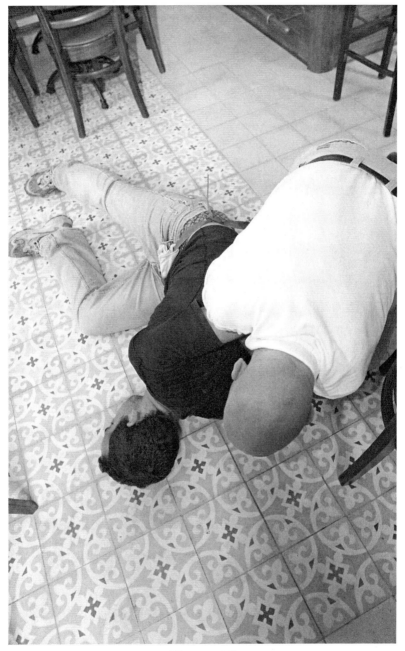

Figure 48

You now have him subdued, but he is still conscious and therefore potentially dangerous. If he is physically stronger than you, then it is only a matter of time before he overpowers you and manages to reach the detonator. You have two choices for your next course of action.

If there are armed civilians or security officers in the area, call them over, explain that you have accosted a suicide bomber, and demand that they shoot him dead. Make sure they go for the head, and pull your head back to avoid getting hit

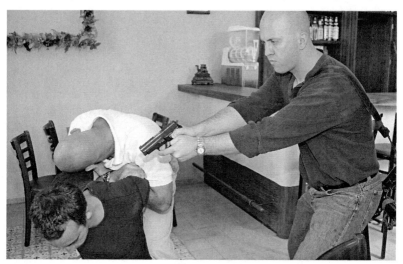

Figure 49

yourself (fig. 49). But chances are you will be alone, abandoned by passersby who fled for their own safety. You will have to kill the terrorist yourself, but without letting go of his arms. Short of head-butting him—which is hardly effective from behind—you will have to deliver a lethal neck bite.

Go for the blood vessels on either side of his neck (fig. 50). They should be plenty visible because of the physical exertion. Bite deeply and viciously. If you manage to reach the carotid artery, the ensuing outpouring of blood should make the terrorist lose consciousness and die within one or two minutes. If not, you will have still damaged a critical set of neck muscles and caused psychological shock, effectively paralyzing him.

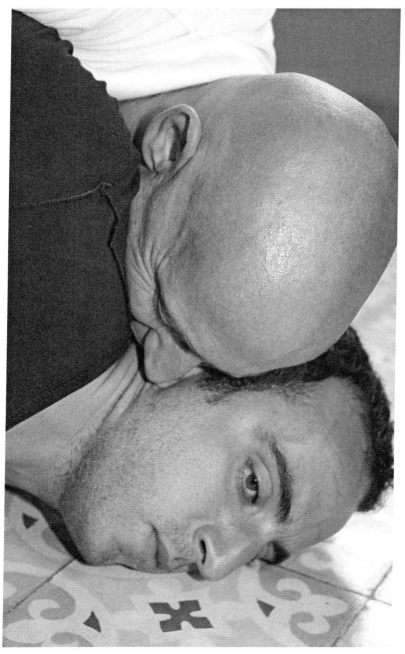

Figure 50

This desperate technique may seem gruesome and even far-fetched to some, but think about it: In this impossible situation, what other choice are you going to have?

BAG BOMBS

While easier to separate from the terrorist than a bomb vest or belt, bombs hidden in bags are in fact riskier because the terrorist will tend to hold the bag tight, with his or her finger directly on the detonator. An exception to this is a backpack, which tends to cause delays in detonation unless the det wires and switch have been laced through the shoulder straps.

If you are about to confront a suicide bomber wearing a backpack, your first job is to note the status of his hands. If they are empty and swinging free, then you can engage him with the technique described above, as though he was wearing a bomb belt. The backpack will make the armlock from behind a little more difficult, but do not hesitate with fear at the thought of explosives pressed directly against your chest. As long as no one reaches the detonator in the struggle, assume that you are safe.

Should the terrorist be walking with his hands on the shoulder straps or positioned toward the bottom of the backpack, or if he is carrying the bomb in a handbag, the options are more limited.

Look for the operative hand—the one carrying the bag or, more likely, the one poised to hit the switch in the backpack. Approach the terrorist from that side. Ignoring the rest of him, aim your strongest punch at the wrist or knuckles of the operative hand. Immediately thereafter, hold his arm in place with your other hand and keep punching at the same spot. Better yet, attack the operative hand with a pocket knife or pen.

The idea is to make the terrorist release the switch before he knows what is going on. The hand is a complex limb—for all its strength, it is also equipped to save itself from harm with a reflex mechanism. The unexpected shock of your punch will hopefully cause the muscles that control the wrist and fingers to contract, opening up the hand.

From there on, it is a face-to-face fight for survival. Once the terrorist releases the detonator, you must lock up his arms as described earlier, preventing him from reaching the switch with either hand. Then use the techniques described in this chapter to finish him off.

Facing a suicide bomber with his or her hand on the detonator is a risky situation to confront, to say the least. As mentioned at the beginning of this chapter, your most realistic option may be to shout a warning to other citizens in the vicinity and then cover up on the ground or dash for close cover.

5

Trigger Unhappy

AMERICANS NEED no introduction to the threat of suicidal shooting sprees. Whether they are the rifles and shotguns of Columbine or the pistol of the Long Island Railroad, guns become indiscriminately lethal in the hands of the sick and aggrieved. Unfortunately, there are too many tales of innocent civilians cowering quietly as a deranged gunman wanders around their building, executing them one by one and saving the last bullet for himself.

The firearm-wielding terrorist creates an identical scenario. There are those in South America, Northern Ireland, the Balkans, and the Palestinian territories who specialize in drive-by shootings or roadside ambushes, with an emphasis on surviving to strike again. But far more effective and terrifying is the kamikaze who draws his weapons while in the heart of a population center, firing point-blank until he is himself killed. Israel alone has seen a half-dozen such attacks by Palestinian gunmen in three years.

In one case, a pistol-packing shoe salesman killed a terrorist rampaging in downtown Tel Aviv, but only after three Israelis had died and another 25 had been wounded. That brave man was lucky to be armed. Most civilians are not willing or able to have the protec-

Columbine High School's all-too-easy atrocity. (Reuters)

M   04/20/98

tion of a privately owned handgun. Even if they are, they may not have the time to reach for it when facing a smoking rifle barrel.

Therefore, the fight-or-flight instinct must be honed in preparation for facing a suicidal gunman.

FLIGHT RISK IS LOWER THEN FREEZE RISK

Flight is the first and best option. A shooter who comes around the corner, into your office, or aboard the public vehicle you are riding might be jumpy, spraying bullets as fast as he can, or slow and methodical as he executes victims one by one. In either scenario, by running in the opposite direction, preferably hunched over and not in a straight line, all the while attempting to put solid and/or visual obstacles between you and the gunman, you will vastly reduce your chances of being hit. If you know there is a chance of escape, go for it. Listen to and respect your fear. Run.

There are no advantages to staying in place with a suicidal gunman on the loose. With a bomb blast, covering up on the ground will increase your chances of survival, but when it comes to an armed attacker who is seeking out victims, the opposite is true. Do not waste time thinking you found "cover." Assume that it does not exist in your average environment. Even the thickest of office furniture won't stop most ammunition at close range. The same goes for train passenger seats, school library bookshelves, and even car doors.

If you are unfortunate enough to get hit by a bullet while you are running away, keep moving! Many, many people have survived even multiple gunshot wounds. It is *not* like TV or the movies, where one shot will send you careening through the air and dump you dead on the pavement. If you are shot, don't stop! Get to a safe location, staunch the bleeding as best you can, and have someone summon medical assistance. Most importantly, *maintain your will to live.*

If you are truly cornered and there is no reasonable avenue of escape, it is time to fight back. Building the will to do so will be one of the hardest acts of your life. The crash of gunshots and the sight of those already felled by bullets will put enormous pressure on your psyche. The temptation to faint or freeze, to submit like a lamb to the slaughter, will be strong.

Fight it, so you can fight the gunman and live. Cherish those eternal seconds of terror not as the last memories of your life but as a chance to crystallize your anger, a springboard into action.

With that in mind, here are your guiding principles when faced by a homicidal gunman:

- Get close enough to grapple with him. Any further away and you're at the mercy of the weapon.
- Go for the hand with the gun, ignoring all other distractions or attacks. As in a knife scenario, the gunman can still attack you with his free hand, so be aware of it; just don't let it distract you from controlling the weapon. During the fight, if an opportunity arises to take a sudden, debilitating strike at a vital target on the gunman's body (such as his throat), do so, but only as long as the attack does not compromise your control of the weapon arm.
- Be aware of where the gun muzzle is pointing at all times. Parry or control the gun so the muzzle does not cross your body in case he manages to squeeze off a shot or there is an accidental discharge during the struggle.
- Be prepared for the shocking effect of gunshots at close distance. Otherwise you are liable to seize up at the sound. Even for those who are used to gunfire from hunting or the shooting range, it can be shocking and disorienting when a gun goes off close to you rather than held out at arm's length, especially without your usual hearing protection in place.

PISTOLS: UP CLOSE AND PERSONAL

Pistol-wielding killers have to get close to their victims for lethal accuracy. Some might even enjoy seeing the fear on their victims' faces before they execute them. This can be made to work to your advantage.

At the gunman's approach, play passive and scared. Cower, beg for your life, and bring up your hands in submission. However, remain in control: stay on your feet, and keep your hands close to your ears rather than spread out wide. If he approaches to within grappling distance, then explode into your counterattack as described below. If he stops short of grappling distance, then you will have to close the gap.

This is obviously a volatile, unpredictable moment, and only you can make the instantaneous decision on how to get close enough to get ahold of the gun. You can shuffle up to him during your cowering act, or you could stumble forward while seemingly crying uncontrollably. In any case, monitor the gunman's behavior and speech carefully. If you cannot get close enough before you think he is about to pull the trigger, you may have to attack suddenly and fiercely or do your best to get past him and escape.

However you manage to get within grappling range, you want to be in a crouch, positioning your head so it (rather than your torso) is in the gun's line of fire (fig. 51). Then, in a burst of action, clamp both hands on the base of the pistol in front of the grip. Force it up (fig. 52) and back (fig. 53), thrusting with your legs for extra leverage. The gunman's trigger finger will be crushed, and his wrist also stands to be damaged unless he releases the pistol immediately. Whatever the case, you have the advantage. You can point the gun

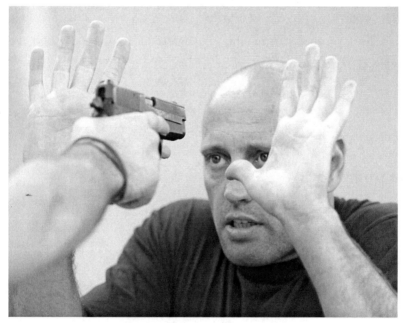

Figure 51

Figure 52

Figure 53

at his head or jam the barrel in his body and hope it goes off (fig. 54). If you feel his grip loosening, you can wrench the weapon from his hands (fig. 55) and turn it on him (fig. 56). Or you can go for close-combat attacks on his knees, shins, groin, stomach, or face.

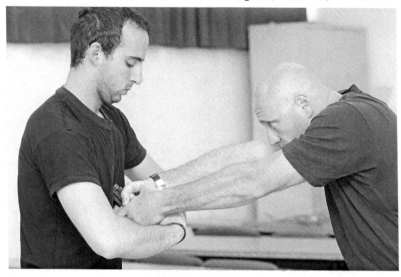

Figure 54

Figure 55

Figure 56

The double-grip technique is not an option, though, if the gunman is pointing at your midriff (fig. 57) because the pistol will not be high enough for you to clear it away in an upward sweep.

Figure 57

Go for the play-acting again to close the distance (fig. 58) and gain the benefit of surprise. When you are within reach of the gunman, leap in the direction of your dominant hand, turning your body sideways so you are out of the line of fire. At the same time, bat or grasp and shove his gun hand with your dominant hand in the opposite direction. The gunman's arm (or arms if he's holding the weapon with two hands) will now be positioned in front of you across your belly (fig. 59).

Figure 58

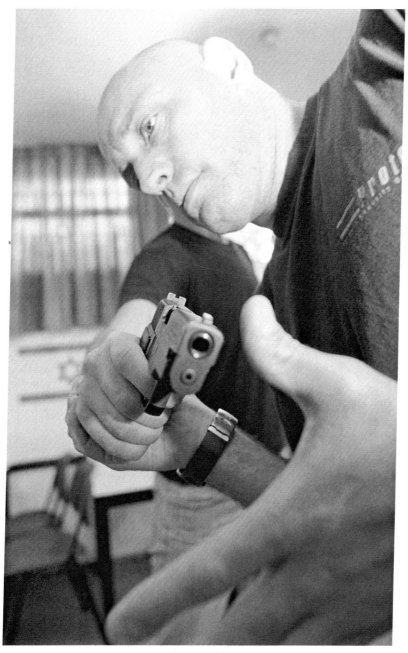

Figure 59

Grab his gun hand by the wrist with your dominant hand. If his gun hand is the one closer to you, stick your dominant elbow into the crook of his elbow for extra stability. Then grab the forward part of the pistol with your other hand (fig. 60) and bend it away from you and against his wrist with full force (fig. 61). The gunman's reflex will be to release the pistol; whether he does so or not, his trigger finger will most likely be crushed in the trigger guard.

Figure 60

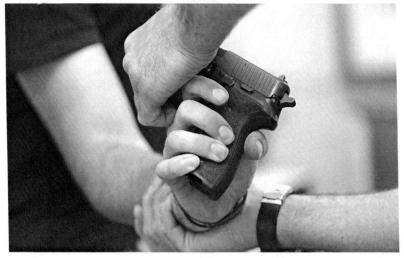

Figure 61

A similar counterattack can be used if the gunman aims at your temple. Raise your hands in mock surrender, either with both of them in front of the pistol's axis (fig. 62) or with the closer hand behind his gun hand (more on this below).

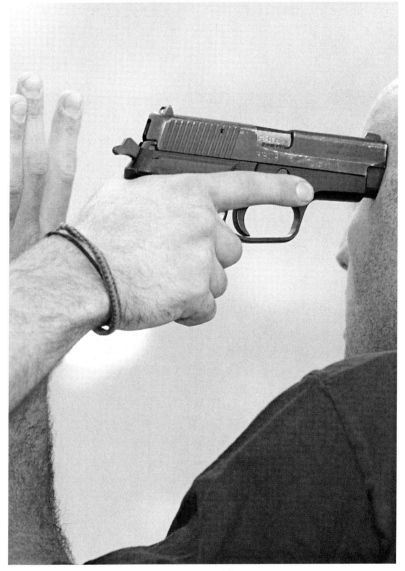

Figure 62

If both your hands are forward, then spin quickly against the pistol arm (fig. 63), turning your head with the spin in the direction of the gunman to clear it from the line of fire. Follow all the way through until your far arm can clamp down hard on his weapon arm as you grasp the gun to control it (fig. 64). Then disarm him as described above by pressuring it against his wrist (fig. 65) and wresting it away (fig. 66). As he resists your counterattack, remain aware of the muzzle's direction at all times!

Figure 63

Figure 64

Figure 65

Figure 66

If your hand is behind his pistol arm (fig. 67), you have two choices. You can quickly grab the pistol and push it forward and away from your head while stepping backward, then go through with the disarm. Or you can bat the pistol down and follow through with an armpit clamp to secure his weapon arm (fig. 68).

Figure 67

THE CITIZEN'S GUIDE TO STOPPING SUICIDE ATTACKERS

Figure 68

With the weapon arm locked in your armpit, you are ready to neutralize the threat. Clamp the gun with one hand while keeping the shooter's wrist in place with your other hand (fig. 69). Then force the gun—and with it, his hand—toward his body with the natural bend of his wrist (fig. 70). If the pain doesn't make him let go, then his stubbornness will work against him: By the time the pistol is turned toward him, his trigger finger may very well have sent a bullet into his own torso.

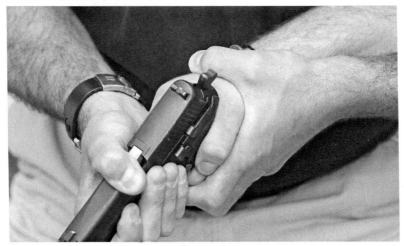

Figure 69

Figure 70

RIFLE: TUG-OF-WAR

A rifleman out to cause carnage is a formidable enemy. As the Beltway sniper showed, such threats are almost impossible to deal with. But if the man in question has a death wish, he may get close enough to confront properly. This is especially true if it is a hostage situation, where terrorists often try to buy time before carrying out their suicidal plans.

Whether the gunman aims his rifle at you from the shoulder or from the hip, he is equally susceptible to being disarmed at close range. The long barrel will enable you to use the power of leverage to your advantage.

Always react in the direction of the gunman's trigger hand. If he is holding the rifle with the butt tucked to his right shoulder (fig. 71), that is your operating side.

Figure 71

As with the pistol scenario, cower and beg, closing the distance between you and the rifle barrel. When you are almost touching, slap or grab and push the rifle barrel to the side opposite his trigger hand while moving your body out of the line of fire (fig. 72). Then grab the barrel with your other hand as you forcefully push the muzzle down and clear of your body as you turn to face the gunman (fig. 73). With your first hand now grasping the rifle stock, yank it toward you while pushing against the barrel with your other hand (fig. 74).

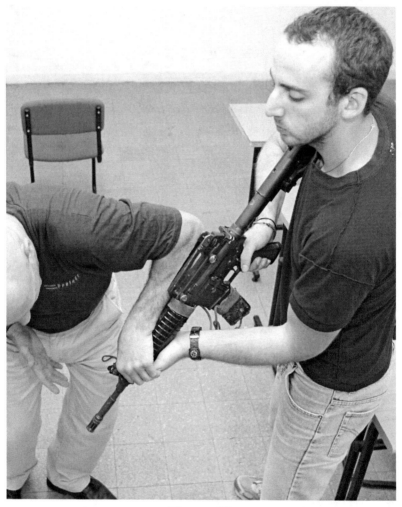

Figure 72

THE CITIZEN'S GUIDE TO STOPPING SUICIDE ATTACKERS

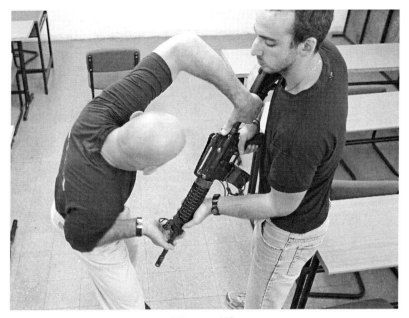

Figure 73

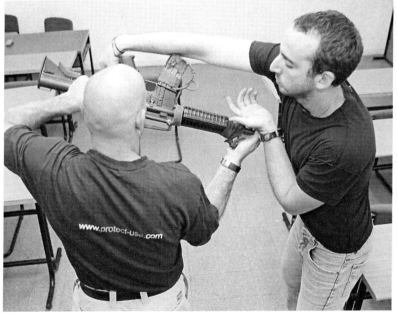

Figure 74

This action will take the gunman by surprise, and you may find yourself armed with his rifle. Turn it on him as a bludgeon (fig. 75), or increase the distance between you and train the weapon on him (fig. 76). If the gunman proves more tenacious and keeps a grip on the gun, pummel him with your knees and elbows, all the while maintaining awareness of the rifle's muzzle direction.

Figure 75

Figure 76

EXECUTION? NO THANKS!

If you find yourself being led away at rifle point, you need no further proof that the time has come to act. In all likelihood, you are being taken away for execution.

Force yourself to slow the pace—even if it means faking a stumble—so that the shooter closes in and you feel the barrel in your back (fig. 77). In a flash, spin all the way around in the direction of the shooter's trigger hand (almost certainly rightward; fig. 78) until the rifle is across your chest. As you come around, reach under the rifle's forward grip with your right arm so that the weapon ends up firmly grasped in the crook of your elbow (fig. 79).

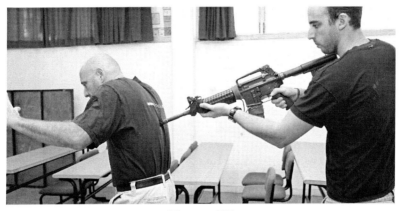

Figure 77

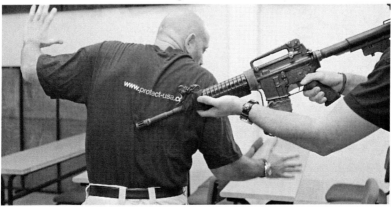

Figure 78

Figure 79

Continue to smash the shooter's face with your left elbow (fig. 80) until you feel his grip on the rifle loosen. Withdraw your left arm, grabbing the rifle stock en route (fig. 81) to sweep the weapon away and bring it to bear on the attacker (fig. 82).

The important point to remember with all suicide gunman scenarios is to get out and stay out of the path of the bullet. That is all you need to get a fighting chance at life.

Figure 80

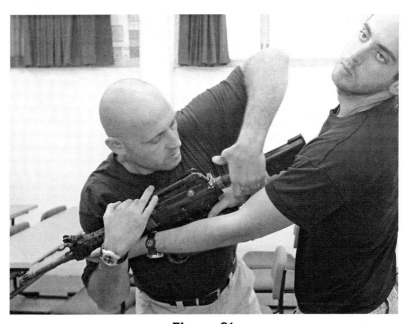

Figure 81

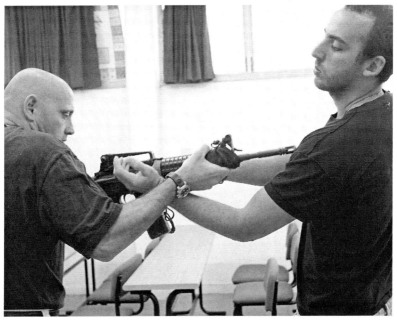

Figure 82

6

Deranged and Deadly

SUBSTANCE ABUSERS and the mentally unsound can turn violent in an instant and put the public in a quandary: How do you deal with a menace who is not legally accountable for his or her actions?

Whether you are a hospital worker handling an injured drunk or simply a civilian in the street who happens to fall afoul of a recently discharged head case, you may well be in mortal danger. The person may not intend to harm you, but he or she may also not be in total control of themselves and as such have no inhibitions. Given the right rush of aggression and the addition of whatever weapon comes to hand, you might be facing someone who by all counts can be considered a suicide attacker.

You must not count on security guards, the police, or passersby to help you. Indeed, sometimes your attacker will seem so pitiful at first that many onlookers will decide that you are the aggressor! Therefore, if you are in a position that entails regular confrontations with potentially hostile people—say, for instance, a hospital emergency room nurse—it is your duty to develop quick-reflex moves that afford you maximum protection while causing minimum injury to someone who could end up demanding compensation. You must also be prepared to take the fight to the next level if the attacker presents a deadly threat.

SACRED SPACE

Everyone has a sacred space, a radius around their body into which they will allow only those they consider trusted intimates. This changes from culture to culture—contrast the in-your-face Mediterranean to nodding-distance Asia. But physical vulnerability is universal, requiring a standard space in which you can more or less guarantee enough reaction time to avoid a blow or more insidious threat, such as a contaminated needle (fig. 83). Arm's length in every direction is about sufficient, more if you sense a potential threat or have an uneasy feeling about someone.

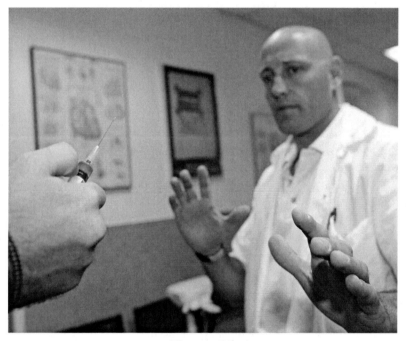

Figure 83

If threatened, put up your hands in a placating gesture, and do not let your potential attacker come through them (fig. 84). In a calm but firm voice, advise the person that he is making you feel threatened and that you do not want a confrontation.

If he persists in pressing the confrontation, back off or run away if you must. You can also grab anything solid to use as a barrier between the two of you. Once you have gone that far, there is no reason not to use your legs as well. Keep him at bay with quick, stabbing kicks, or place the sole of your foot on his thigh or pelvis in a braking move (fig. 85). Be ready to forcefully retract your foot if he attempts to grab and twist it. Whether kicking or bracing him

Figure 84

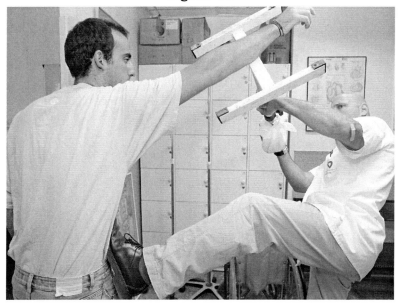

Figure 85

with your leg, also be ready for any sudden, determined rush to topple you backward. Always mind your balance!

A quick exit to call a security guard or police officer is ideal but not always possible. You may find yourself boxed in before you can escape, or you may not want to leave other, less capable people than yourself as the next in line to be menaced. So if your would-be attacker has not backed down, it is time to step in.

Your focus is going to be on the hand closet to you (e.g., the one he's using to point at you or grab your clothing). The next time he threatens you with it, deflect it in toward him so that his elbow is about at your chest level (fig. 86). Firmly grab his wrist and elbow. While continuing to defuse his aggressiveness verbally, push him toward the nearest wall. The pressure you apply should be enough to keep him off balance while you take him sideways. Then pin him to the wall and hold him there until you can de-escalate the situation or help arrives.

If he proves strong enough to shove you back, use his momentum against him. Step back with him while still holding on and then spin him around, looking over your shoulder for a fixed object to pin him against.

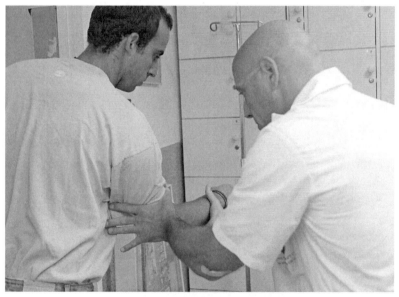

Figure 86

TOUCH TACTIC

What if you are caught by surprise? Even the most innocuous of conversations can turn violent when your interlocutor is deranged or under intense stress. He might want you to "get the point," which means the classic grab at your lapels to pull you close to his face.

Obviously, this is in direct violation of your personal space, and you could be forgiven for wanting to use the disabling moves we outlined earlier in this book. Only you can tell if such a response is warranted. But remember that you are not dealing with a hardened terrorist who is committed to killing you. A less injurious but just as effective move may be the right choice to win back your sacred space.

Reach forward and poke your attacker just under the larynx (fig. 87). Use your index and middle finger, curving them down into his clavicle. Make it a slow poke; a thrust could fatally crush his vocal cords. His reaction will be a full-body gag reflex of sorts, and he will back off instantly. Best of all, to all onlookers—and potential witnesses—you will appear to have merely touched the man.

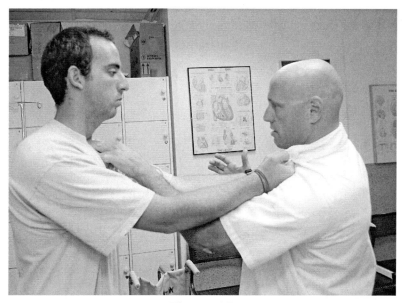

Figure 87

TEAMWORK

For truly menacing characters, it might still be worth using the nonlethal approach, especially if you have backup. Hospital staffers should make a point of practicing various code words and signals that will alert one another to the need for a combined effort to subdue a threat.

The best method to handle these situations is also the most instinctive—each staffer locks down a different set of limbs.

Whoever approaches the attacker from behind should go for the legs (fig. 88)—otherwise he'll just try to kick you away if you try to grab his legs in full view from the front. Grab him at the knees and press them together, like a rugby tackle. The second staffer then bear-hugs the man, pinning his arms to his flanks (fig. 89). It is wise to try to position yourself low and to the aggressor's side rather than his front in order to limit his ability to bite you.

Once the attacker is in your combined grasp, the staffer at his legs should pull them off the floor while the other one eases him to the ground. Once prostrate he will be easier to deal with, but take no chances. Both staffers should kneel on him, using body-

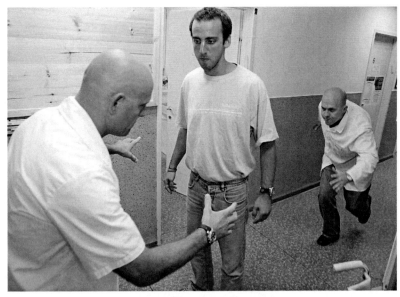

Figure 88

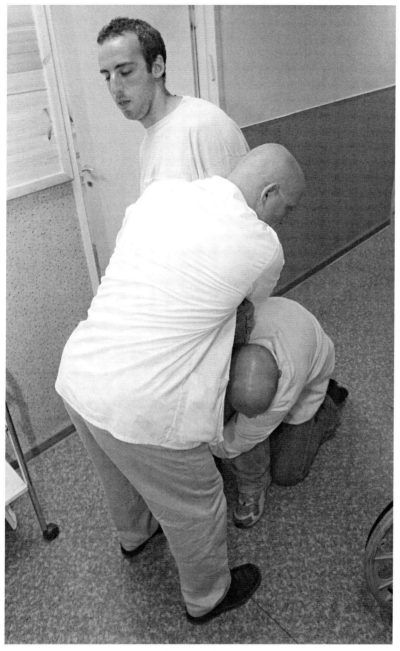

Figure 89

weight to keep him immobile (fig. 90). The topmost staffer should also hold down his head to prevent him from biting or bashing himself against the floor.

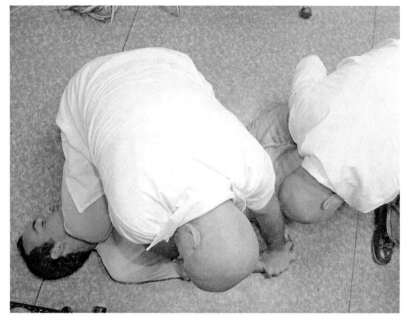

Figure 90

7

Car Trouble

A TERRORIST with mayhem on his mind or a psycho with an axe to grind need look no further than his own automobile for a weapon of mass destruction. A ton of steel and glass barreling down on unwary pedestrians has the killing power of heavy ordnance. In February 2001, a Palestinian bus driver mowed down a crowd at Azur junction in southern Israel. Eight Israelis were killed, and the bus driver kept going until police blew out his tires during a hot pursuit.

The carnage of an intentional car attack rivals most any other murder method known to man. The scenario has been repeated in war zones and peaceful areas. Of course, sometimes it is the result of a driver who simply lost control of the car and jumped the curb, as was seen with the horrible incident at the Farmers Market in Santa Monica, California, in the summer of 2003.

Unfortunately, the ordinariness of vehicles in almost every setting means that detection and evasion is difficult. Forget all those kung-fu hijinks of jumping over the roof or lying flat at the last moment so the car passes over you. Such stunts defy the laws of gravity and human reflex. There is no fending off a high-speed fender.

Azur junction after the bus hit-and-run in February 2001.
(Associated Press)

THE CITIZEN'S GUIDE TO STOPPING SUICIDE ATTACKERS

As a pedestrian, you must remember that prevention is far, far better than cure. Treat the threat of car attack as you would a bomber or shooter looking for a concentration of potential victims by avoiding crowds at roadsides. That also means giving up on those charming curbside cafes, be they on Melrose Avenue or the Champs Elysee. The advent of al-Qaeda means you can no longer take safety for granted with such proximity to traffic.

Obviously you cannot avoid roads entirely, so developing an instinct for positioning is key. Always place a fixed object between yourself and oncoming cars. Street- or traffic-light pylons are good, as are those heavy-duty mailboxes. These objects might not totally stop a careening car, but they might slow one down enough for you to reach safety or at least provide an apparent obstacle between you and the driver that he will try to avoid. Newspaper dispensers and garbage cans are less reliable for this, as these are rarely fastened to the ground securely. Trees can also deceive— robust as they look, they may have been recently planted by city hall and not have the roots necessary to absorb impact fully.

Although you'd have to move quick, rushing into a nearby store or building, especially if it is made of brick or something equally solid, is another option. If you do this, keep running to the back to put as much of the building's structure as possible between you and the car.

Besides paying attention to your positioning, keep your ears open too. If you hear screeching tires or the sudden acceleration of a car engine, don't take it for granted. Look around to find its source, and be ready to dart to safety.

But if, despite all this, you still find yourself in the path of an oncoming vehicle, the best you can do is leap aside as quickly as possible. The shock of a car's sideswipe is far more survivable than a full-front impact. And a good dive could clear your head and vital organs, leaving your legs to take the blow. Painful, yes, but better than instant death.

8

Fight or Sit Tight?

SO FAR WE have dealt with the nightmare scenario of facing a terrorist mere seconds away from killing you in a suicide attack. But imagine those seconds being stretched into minutes, hours, or even days. That is what happens when the terrorists decide to go for a double whammy—taking hostages and thereby reaping maximum publicity before hitting the switch for a spectacular and bloody conclusion.

In October 2002, Chechen guerrillas strolled onto the stage of a Moscow theater as a musical was in full swing. By the time the 800 audience members realized it was not part of the show, it was too late. The standoff with Russian authorities lasted three days. Finally, after the Chechens shot a hostage dead, the Russians went in—hard. Fearing that the 40-odd hostage takers would bring the house down with their cache of 300 pounds of explosives, special forces neutralized them before storming in by flooding the theater with gas 100 times more powerful than morphine. The Chechens were quickly killed, but around 200 hostages also died from inhaling too much of the airborne narcotic.

In purely professional terms, the rescue operation was a suc-

Chechen terrorists, hostages at hand, give a televised statement during a 2002 standoff. (Associated Press)

МОСКВА, ул.МЕЛЬНИКОВА

cess. After all, the 25 percent hostage fatality rate was vastly preferable to the absolute devastation the terrorists would have wreaked by going kamikaze. But that is little consolation to those who fell victim to one of history's more extreme cases of "friendly fire."

Could the hostages have done anything to save themselves? Yes. And while the chances of success are slim, they are always better than just lying down to die at some criminal's discretion.

SEIZE THE FRAY

There are two critical stages of a hostage situation: the terrorist takeover and the rescue attempt by security forces. (Remember: Suicide attackers are not looking for a peaceful resolution.) Both stages are violent, but their dynamics are different.

In the first, the terrorists will cow hostages into submission, resorting to lethal force only in exceptional cases. In the second, the SWAT team will do everything possible to remain covert until they come in with blinding speed, killing anyone seen as hostile. This means that, if you are going to run for it, the initial takeover is your only feasible opportunity.

"The terrorists rely on surprise to capture as many hostages as possible, as quickly as possible," said Assaf Heffetz, a former chief of the Israel Police, founder of its SWAT team, and now a security adviser with the international TIX Group. "Their priority is gathering together as controllable a group as possible, so those who run away immediately have a good chance of not being noticed."

You will know the takeover has been completed when the commotion stops. Hostages—yourself included—will be rounded up and most likely forced to sit in a position that makes flight difficult, probably on the floor. (In the Moscow theater, audience members were simply told to stay in their seats, with guards posted in the aisles.) Blindfolds will likely follow. The terrorists will deploy through the room or building, sealing exits, choosing ideal lookout spots, then telephoning the outside world to announce their "triumph." As far as you are concerned, escape is no longer an option.

Since plane, bus, and train hijackings became a favored terrorist tactic in the late 1960s, there have been instances where hostages managed to get away despite the odds. During negotiations, security teams have always stayed close to the heart of the action in case a hardy civilian slipped out of a window to freedom while his captors were distracted. But with the new primacy of suicide terrorism, this must now be seen as the exception, not the rule. The Irish Republican Army (IRA) or Red Brigades never wore bomb belts that could be set off at the touch of a button, and they considered self-sacrifice a last resort rather than an objective in itself. And of course, for today's suicide terrorists your life is less than worthless, so do not expect that your alleged value as a "bargaining chip" will save your life.

So once the hostage takers are in control, you had best settle down unless an absolutely clear opportunity for escape presents itself. Could be that the one gunman watching over your group of hostages is suddenly cut down by a silenced SWAT sniper shot. Could be that, while being taken to the bathroom, you manage to dash out a previously unnoticed emergency exit. Just be aware that, if you misjudge your chances and do not succeed, you will be killed outright. And even if you do succeed, it may provoke the terrorists into unleashing their wrath on the hostages left behind.

GO GRAY

So there you are, bunched up with a dozen strangers under the guns of masked fanatics just waiting for an excuse to hit the trigger. There's a chance that they will first want to execute a hostage or two to show the authorities they are serious and score some serious television airtime.

At this point, heroics are out of the question. You must now become the opposite of a hero, doing everything possible to be unremarkable to the terrorists. Security experts call it "going gray."

Avoid eye contact with the terrorists, and as much as possible keep your gaze locked on the floor. If addressed by the terrorists, look at their throat or upper chest area when answering. This will appear deferential and unthreatening to them, but it will still give you a chance to gather important tactical details for possible later use. (Are he and his comrades dressed in civilian clothes or uniforms? Is he wearing webbing with extra ordnance such as another firearm or grenades? How about a bomb belt or a remote detonator for a bomb planted elsewhere?)

If you are a man of athletic build, play it down. Assume a slumped posture. Keep long sleeves on. The hostage takers will be looking for any early signs of possible resistance to put down. This is especially true if the terrorists are of Middle Eastern origin, as they tend to be smaller in build than Western men and will therefore be eager to assert their physical control of the situation by using force.

If you are a woman of any age between 16 and 60, beware of actions that could be misinterpreted as flirtatious. Terrorists tend to come from conservative cultures where women are either idealized or demeaned or both. (Some of the 9/11 hijackers reportedly partied at strip clubs the night before the attack, leaving behind notes berating women as "whores.") There is mounting evidence that suicide terrorists act, in part, out of a distorted code of religious chastity. So even an innocent gesture by a female hostage, like removing a jacket if the room gets too hot, could draw the wrath of a bad guy convinced she is out to deprive him of his 72 virgins in paradise.

And what of women terrorists who are becoming more and more common? The rule of making yourself appear undistinguished applies doubly to them, especially because hostages are liable to assume a woman captor is more merciful or malleable.

"Women terrorists are extra dangerous," said a hostage negotiator who, for operational security reasons, gave his name as Alex. "Most of them had to fight the prejudices of their own people to achieve the status of fighter and will jump at the opportunity to prove they are more ruthless than their comrades. They view male hostages as oppressors, women hostages as weak and contemptible."

Politics are behind 99 percent of all terrorist acts, and though it will probably take you a while to learn what exactly is motivating your captors, there is no need to invite risk. Dump any religious symbols (skullcaps, crucifix pendants, etc.) as soon as possible. Do not react to any ethnic slurs the terrorists spout. Talk yourself into believing they are not so different from you, as this will help you stave off the mental paralysis often caused by an unfamiliar menace.

The terrorists will want to collect passports and IDs almost immediately to see who they have taken hostage and ascertain their value. Unfortunately, documents do not lie, so you must think fast. Radical Muslims long ago declared open season on Americans and Israelis, and terrorists elsewhere in the Third World have followed suit to protest U.S. "imperialism." Thanks to the United Kingdom's involvement in both Gulf Wars, the British are no longer safe either. And citizens of Western nations are not the only targets. Chechens and their sympathizers target Russians. Citizens of Singapore are viewed with some hostility by the Muslim states of Southeast Asia, and the al Qaeda-linked cells there are likely to ratchet this up into terrorist attacks.

If your home nation has enemies with terrorist histories, you should be prepared. At the very least, try to get rid or your passport (e.g., toss it out a window, slip it under floorboards, rip it up and flush it down a toilet) and try to bluff your way through subsequent questioning. If you want to be especially well prepared, you can equip yourself with dummy documents available from various companies. These can be outright forgeries of passports from countries considered safe or neutral (e.g., Canada, Ireland, Switzerland) or the real thing left over from countries that no longer exist (e.g., Rhodesia). Either should be good enough to pass inspection by a stressed-out terrorist. The legality of carrying such documents is questionable—a risk vs. reward calculation you must make in advance.

At the very least, carry a second wallet with some small bills and less important cards. You can offer this to the terrorists, claiming that it is all you carry when you are out and about. Fill in other details of your identity as you see fit, but it is wise to have thought about a plausible fake story beforehand.

LISTEN, LEARN

Acting submissive does not mean thinking like a hostage. Now that the standoff is underway, whether it lasts hours or days, you have a duty to stay alert and improve your chances of surviving.

You will most likely be searched at the outset of the takeover. As mentioned above, the terrorists will be looking for documents as well as anything that can obviously be used as a weapon.

If you have a cell phone, try to stay in possession of it. Stick it down the back of your pants if necessary. One of the hostages in the Moscow theater was, unbeknownst to the Chechens, an agent from the FSB (the former KGB). Throughout the three-day siege, he managed to pass on invaluable intelligence with his cell phone. The man told the Russians that the two main bombs in the auditorium and on the balcony were not armed. To set them off, the female suicide bombers needed more than a minute to connect the batteries to the detonators. That crucial information gave the SWAT team the confidence to go in.

Do the same if possible—but first, turn down the ring volume to zero to avoid detection if someone happens to call you. It should be enough to dial the police emergency number and simply whisper details; it will be recorded. Using a cellular messaging system like SMS is even better, as it is quiet and clear.

Once you have a channel of communication open, make sure you pass on the correct information.

"There are two main things that interest a SWAT team commander at a hostage takeover: the number of terrorists and what ordnance they have at their disposal," said Heffetz. "Information about the hostages—their number, condition, what have you—is really secondary. Whether there are four or 40, we still plan to get them out, and the terrorists are still going to put up a fight over them."

There have been cases of hostages being taken outside by their captors during negotiations and using the opportunity to get out information with hand signals. Beware this method. Today's crises are covered avidly by live television, and every move you make could be picked up and broadcast worldwide—including into the terrorists' own den.

LANGUAGE AND LIES

As the standoff drags on, you will likely find yourself exposed in some way to negotiation efforts. At the very least, you will hear the authorities calling on your captors with loudspeakers outside until they establish a telephone connection. If you are lucky, you will get to hear the captors' response.

Your instinct will be to listen for signs of agreement and a resolution in the making. This is a waste of time because, in reality, you have no control over such things. Far more important is whether there are inconsistencies between what the captors tell the authorities and how they behave among themselves. Do they exaggerate or play down their number? Do they misrepresent the amount of weaponry they have on hand? Are they hysterical on the phone but calm in person, or vice-versa?

"Any hostage negotiator knows that the key to a happy end is establishing some sort of trust, credibility with the hostage takers. If they are lying, then it bodes very badly indeed for everyone concerned, because it indicates they really don't want to get out alive," Alex said.

If you are in contact with the authorities, send out as quickly as possible clarifications to lies told by the terrorists concerning themselves or their weapons. Otherwise, carefully spread the knowledge among the other hostages that your captors are likely suicidal. You run the risk of starting a panic, but in the post-9/11 world, where every good citizen knows that it is worth putting up a fight rather than submitting to politically motivated murder, you will also identify your comrades should it come down to a desperate last-ditch effort to attack the terrorists yourselves.

All of the above assumes that the terrorists are speaking your language. If not, then your options are especially limited. But even in the face of this obstacle, you can still stay vigilant for things like rituals or a noticeable change in behavior. Islamist terrorists, for example, are known to play recordings of Arabic worship to steel themselves for the final battle. It is a distinctive noise, not something that could be confused with pop music. There is also the possibility of last-minute bullying by the terrorists as they look to you for provocation to give them an excuse to hit the switch.

If any sign indicates an impending deadly action by your captors, the time has come to fight back. With as many fellow hostages as you have recruited, charge the terrorists and give them everything you have. Focus on the leaders or those who are carrying the triggers to bombs. As on an airplane, use your superiority of numbers and the principle of mass assault to overwhelm the enemy. Always be alert for improvised weapons to use in a last-ditch assault—heavy chairs, fire extinguishers (as both an impact and chemical weapon), and kitchen utensils are only some of the possibilities.

A tactical unit storms a hijacked Berlin bus last April. Dynamic entries mean more risk for the unprepared hostage. (Reuters)

THE CITIZEN'S GUIDE TO STOPPING SUICIDE ATTACKERS

SURVIVING SWAT

Long before you reach this point, however, the local SWAT team will have almost certainly had a go at freeing you. That is just the nature of tactical units: because they are well funded and trained, their commanders are eager for a chance to put the boys through a real operation. In fact, many standoffs see as much friction between the SWAT chief and politicians as between the authorities and the terrorists.

As far as you are concerned, this means a tactical assault sooner, rather than later, than you expected.

So-called "Israeli style" entries are now common with SWAT teams all over the world. The shooters come into the room screaming "Everybody down!" Those who do not obey are assumed to be terrorists and shot. For this reason, do not under any circumstances rise up and run when the shooting starts.

The best position is a low squat, leaning one shoulder against a wall, with your hands clasped in front of you. With the wall to brace you and your knees flexed, you will have enough control to adjust your position should the situation require it. Keeping your empty hands in full view will identify you as a non-threat to the SWAT team members as they scan over you. This position will also afford you some flexibility to avoid full exposure to incapacitating gas should the SWAT team use it, especially if it is introduced through the floor as was done in the Moscow theater raid.

There have been situations in which terrorists have grabbed hostages to use as human shields. If this happens to you, do not scream or overly resist. It will make the terrorist more likely to shoot you in his desperate, agitated state. Instead, just go limp. Your body will become dead weight, and as soon as the terrorist tries to move or bring his weapon to bear on a SWAT member, you will fall away, hopefully to safety.

About the Authors

Itay Gil is the founder and chief executive officer of Protect, a Jerusalem-based security training firm (www.protect-usa.com). He spent his compulsory military service in Israel's paratrooper reconnaissance company, serving in the 1982 Lebanon War. He then joined the elite counterterrorist unit Yamam and took part in hundreds of hostage-rescue and interdiction missions. Gil later became the Yamam's chief close-quarter combat instructor, drawing on his 20 years' martial arts experience. From 1992 to 1997, he was the executive director of all training programs for the Israeli Border Police and undercover police intelligence units.

Gil continues to serve in the Israel Defense Forces (IDF) reserves as senior combat instructor for the undercover counter-terrorism unit 217 (Sayeret Duvdevan). In 2002, Gil formed a special security team for the Israeli Defense Ministry.

Gil's methods for dealing with suicide bombers have been documented on CNN, Fox, and Israeli media.

Dan Baron is a Boston-based writer specializing in security issues. Previous experiences include "script doctoring" in Hollywood and researching doomsday cults and the police weapons industry in the United States.

Original photography by *Gil Cohen-Magen*.